Museum of Kindness

Museum
of Kindness

Susan Elmslie

Brick Books

Library and Archives Canada Cataloguing in Publication

Elmslie, Susan, author
        Museum of kindness / Susan Elmslie.

Poems.
Issued in print and electronic formats.
ISBN 978-1-77131-467-1 (softcover).—ISBN 978-1-77131-469-5 (PDF).—
ISBN 978-1-77131-468-8 (EPUB)

        I. Title.

PS8559.L62M87 2017   c811'.54   C2017-902793-X
                                               C2017-902794-8

We acknowledge the Government of Canada, the Canada Council for the Arts, and
the Ontario Arts Council for their support of our publishing program.

The author photo was taken by Wes Folkerth.
The book is set in Minion Pro.
The cover image is "Simon-Geai-Bleu" by René Bolduc, used by his kind permission.
Design and layout by Marijke Friesen.
Printed and bound by Sunville Printco Inc.

Brick Books
431 Boler Road, Box 20081
London, Ontario N6K 4G6

www.brickbooks.ca

Kan hende jeg seiler min skute på grunn;
men så er det dog deilig å fare!

And what if I did run my ship aground;
oh, still it was splendid to sail it!

—Henrik Ibsen

For Masarah Van Eyck

CONTENTS

Material
Box   / 1
Crossing Over   / 2
The Tenants   / 3
To Mark the Day I Saw I Could Slip This Skin   / 5
Poetry   / 6
Convalescent   / 7
Genre   / 8
Faith Is a Suitcase   / 10
Legacy   / 11
A Poet Has Nine Knives   / 12
But the mob all calls me "Swingin'-Door Susie"   / 13
Material   / 14

Trigger Warning
School Shooting   / 17
untitled (bullet)   / 18
Unteachable Moment   / 19
Now you can turn your personal gear into an on-the-go
   bullet-proof shield   / 21
If   / 22
Trigger Warning   / 24
There is never just one trauma, the therapist says   / 26
Teaching Philosophy, Revised   / 28
In Retrospect   / 30
Conventions   / 32
Blooms for Anastasia   / 33
The Worst   / 35

Threshold

Event Horizon   / 39

In Praise of Hospital Cafeterias   / 41

Adventures in Microgravity   / 43

Nightmare   / 45

Strict Bed Rest   / 46

Fury to Bed Rest   / 48

Gift Horse   / 49

New Father's Guidebook, A-Z   / 50

My Daughter, Crying Herself to Sleep   / 51

I wanted to watch my own caesarean and see you born   / 52

Threshold   / 53

Ativan   / 54

Descent   / 55

Miracle   / 56

After the diagnosis I went to the pool to ease into
    cold fact   / 58

Broken Baby Blues   / 59

Happy Blues   / 60

Going Under   / 62

First Outing with Adaptive Stroller   / 64

At the Ophthalmologist's   / 65

Grammar of a Sleep Disorder   / 67

For Magnus, at Seven   / 68

After Meeting with the School Psychologist   / 70

Quick   / 72

Going Under II   / 74

Alive   / 76

Grass   / 78

Museum of Kindness

My First Daughter   / 81

Charles Darwin on His Namesake,
    Charles Waring Darwin   / 83

Mark Twain, December 25, 1909, on the Death of
    His Daughter Jean, Who Drowned in a Bathtub
    During a Seizure   / 85

Icarus, in Therapy   / 87

Eve, in the Garden   / 88

Pandora @ Snoops Anon.   / 89

Babysat by Sylvia Plath   / 90

Glenn Gould's Chair   / 91

Cry   / 92

Sponge, on a Shelf Beside the Bath   / 93

Violet   / 94

Sex at Thirty-Eight   / 95

Happy New Ear   / 96

Brisking about the Life   / 97

Museum of Kindness   / 98

Idyll   / 103

Rosary   / 104

Bonne Continuation   / 105

Acknowledgements and Notes   / 109

Material

Box

Big enough for me to crawl into. It might've held
a fake Christmas tree, neighbour's TV or holiday
imperishables from the Sally Ann.
I was ten, making a house in the living room.

Cut out a window, opened a door. "Look at my box,"
I called to my mother, and her friend put down his drink,
chided, half-slurred, "Don't say that," in a tone
that begged me to ask why. "Don't say

that," he said again. And in the pause
while he raised his glass in slow-mo and drank,
eyeing me, I sat back on my heels and glimpsed
the fourth wall, a spare self watching a trashy play.

"Cut it out," my mother said, "she's just a kid," swatting
the wasp after the sting. "I'm just a fucking drunk," his line.
Everything doubled, obscene, sublime—
No safety in words, then. And more room.

Crossing Over

I drove my ten-speed to the dingy salon,
drawn by the sign: *Special! $10 Perm!*
                        I wanted: loose,
moussed, wavy-on-the-way-to-
corkscrew. Body, movement. To be reborn.
I'd torn out an ad for Tampax—a blonde,
tanned, wearing tennis whites, curls buoyant
and backlit as she lunged close to the net.
No sweat. Eyes on the ball.

The small room was faded pink.
Sink, cracked. The hairdresser, named Marlene
or Noreen—I didn't catch it—spilled solution
down my neck. Fumes stoned me. Ruined my
I'm on a sea food diet: I see food, I eat it T-shirt.

"There it is, hon" she said, squinting,
holding the mirror,
a black-ringed halo, behind my head.
                        "Only thirteen?"
Maureen probed (rankled or pleased?).
In my palm she planted rosary beads.

The Tenants

"You should have kicked them out when he put Ajax
on her steak." Betty weighing in,
Betty who has mynah birds and listens to talk
radio all day, drone of male voices colourless as gin.
"And her pregnant."
"You're not so hot yourself!" Beautiful the mynah squawks
from her cage in the dining room.

An ambulance had come and taken Mrs. Q.
No siren. She was home within a week.
"Should have kicked them out *then!*"
Betty shushes herself dramatically; her finger,
a furious metronome, blurs pursed lips.
"And to torch *your* basement
for the insurance on *his* things!"

"Will Daddy come back
now that we don't have a house?" my brother whines.

Mother isn't talking,
there's a smouldering ring
where her face should be
as she digs in the garbage bag of donated clothes
to find a sweater for my brother. I cling
to my house-coat because I wore it on the curb
watching firemen squelch the flames.

Beautiful shrieks in her cage.
Days and weeks I watch men rebuild our house
from my perch on Betty's couch.
Mom must be in court or conked out on tranqs. "*Shush—*"
Betty hushes the birds and the news spews like ash

from the radio on her fridge. No one else speaks.
At night, we doze on the pull-out in Betty's basement
where two full suits of armour keep watch by the bar.

To Mark the Day I Saw I Could Slip This Skin

for Billy

"That's impossible," I sneered at my brother, one
Saturday spent bantering in front of the TV.

The remark that sparked such incredulity in me
is lost to the darning pile of memory,

along with my sundry worn-out resentments from
growing up the scrawny four-eyed baby of the family.

Though I do clearly remember his reply,
sing-song, prepackaged: "Nothing's impossible,"

in a tone somewhere between Mom's pep talk
and the mischief-nicked baritone of Jack Palance

hosting *Ripley's Believe It or Not.*
I had to bite:

"Some things are. A snake driving a car."
I thought I had him, but he didn't skip a beat,

he pointed at the TV, which was showing a cartoon.
And without a thread of triumph, impossibly cool,

he said, "Look," just as a snake hopped into a car,
coiled about the steering wheel, and sped out of sight.

Poetry

Only embroidery and cancer are slower,
sometimes not even.

The blending
of punishment

and reward.
Can't pay someone

to do it well.
Russian ballet and break dance,

waltz and lap dance,
champagne and bathtub gin.

Lashing
and balm.

Convalescent

I think: if I am dying then I will want to go to the beach.
Someone will prop me on a chaise longue
(I even like hearing the words *chaise longue*)
under a canvas umbrella snapping like rigging in the wind,
facing the ocean, of course. I'll drink Evian
(liquid yoga, my friend calls it) from a glass
with a bendy straw. I see a hand,
not my own, supporting that glass
and another adjusting the pillow behind my head.
Then my friend begins to slice me an Alabama peach.

What does this mean? I'm sure it's neurotic
to devour convalescence as a genre.
It's not so bad, my friend says: It means
you're always getting better.
Means you're already past the worst.

Genre

for Masarah

When I met you, you were School
for the Performing Arts—always rehearsal,
never roses, and you just wanted someone
to say *Go straight to makeup.*
I was Jumble Sale, recovering
discarded parts of myself, digging
through nests of linen tablecloths and silk
scarves, holding them up to the light
to see the reason someone had let them go.
Then you were Xanax in Aix
and I was Addicted to Wool Blankets
(the dissertating years, fuck 'em). Funny
how, after that, my genre was Convalescence—
mountains, lounge chair, letters by post
sealed with wax, and you were Prodigal Child,
Sunday dinners at the parents' with the good boy
med student. When you found the Cartier box
with the one-carat solitaire, you were not
Bridezilla, not Trophy Wife. You
were Bear Chews off Its Own Paw. We visited
the zoo in Madison, saw the tiger mark its territory
and the camel chew its cage, and were reruns
of our fantasy cooking show—
Ancient Mariner Cuisine—over wine, quail,
and a bonfire. We looked forward
to being Flowered Numbers in Greece,
but I became Prenatal Yoga, then
Wears My Brest Friend Nursing Pillow™ as Life Vest
and you—actually this is a black hole for me—
I think you were Doing It Right with Rona

8

the Therapist and I was pretty much Daily Grind,
lacking imagination at the competitive level.
Water Under the Bridge, I hope.
You encouraged me to be Honkytonk, purge
my closet, and get some therapy. I urged you
toward Thongify Your Panty Lines, made you take me
dancing and drive me home in my car from the airport.
Then it was Mimosas at Dawn and Apricot Pastries.
Since your car crash, you've wavered
somewhere between Frida Kahlo and Ironic
Motivational Poster (*Meetings: None of us
is as dumb as all of us*). But I know
the pain is its own genre, and thank God
for your real-life Handyman, who holds you
and builds things, and doesn't lose his head
in your parents' Country Club.
Even before my youngest's diagnosis,
beginning with the five months of bed rest,
you've searched the horizon with binoculars;
I've been Junk-Raft Son of Town Hall,
crossing the North Atlantic: squall, albatross,
roiling sea serpents. I don't know
how this poem ends, but I'm so done
with Unintentional Ombré; I'm off
to get highlights, which I hope are more
Gisele Bündchen than Carol Brady.

Faith Is a Suitcase

You've lugged it
down narrow aisles,
hoisted and stowed it overhead
with the ersatz pillows,

leaned on it
during the layover, dozed,
head nodding like a monk at prayer.

Hello split seam, wonky wheel.
Who wouldn't blame the gorilla?

Locked, key lost. It waits
in the corner of the room
like an agèd aunt.

Legacy

My Granny slit her wrists to get away
from Gramps, said she
was happy just to stroll across the even lawn of the home,
have her own bed.
>"What a *coup*," I said
>when I got the skinny from Mom, at twenty,
>over perfect tea and scones (my own secrets
>deadheaded, swept into the bin).

She introduced me to death, was the first
person I knew to die. Of natural causes,
when I was five.

Wilhelmina Brown.

Your wee
lass is grown.
She handles knives,
is sharpening.

A Poet Has Nine Knives

One to trim the fat
One to cut the line
One for father's back
One for that crook Time
One to keep it sharp
And to slice it thin
One that's sly and jagged
As a gutted tin
One for keeping sheathed
One to pick the latch
One whose only deed's
To carve your epitaph

But the mob all calls me "Swingin'-Door Susie"

Think I'll grow up to be one of you, just another
Sue? Name like a whisper, half a sneeze,
pig call. In Chinese: plain. In French: drunk.
Pocket change. See you in court.

Material

I prefer the absurdity of writing poems / to the absurdity of not
writing poems.
—Wislawa Szymborska, "Possibilities"
(trans. Stanisław Barańczak & Clare Cavanagh)

"At least you got a poem out of it,"
we'd say, thin on irony, as though
getting a poem out of it absolved you
of schtupping a married man,
failing your comps, losing
your rent at the slots.

Now, years on, careworn,
doesn't it seem quaint
to be consoled by getting a poem out of it,
whatever it is? Dividend of grief.
One of the perks of pain. Gifted
with an endless supply of material,
redemption only a roundel away.

Trigger Warning

School Shooting

Dawson College, September 13, 2006

for my daughter

When shots blanched the corridors and a small throng
of students and another teacher crouched on my office floor,
some under desks, some receiving calls or text-messages
until I commanded, "Turn off phones in case they give us away,"
there was an instant, between the first shot that ruptured the silence
and our release by the swat team that chalked an x on my door,
that I met the dark eyes of the girl nearest me and beheld
you—and knew whatever happened to me it'd be
all right, your dad, harrowed, would raise you, I'd live
in memory, fading with time, all right. I felt
from one side what looked like faith and,
from the other, unforgivable: I could go
true as a tree felled by lightning.
Not as one who parts seas but as one who splits,
child of a God who seems to have abandoned us perfectly,
and can do no wrong.

•

I can tell you there is a static silence
between reports of a gun; bullets

pierce drywall; we were too afraid to move
a filing cabinet to block the door;

when the smooth-jawed SWAT officer
ordered me to hold it open for my students

then swung around to cover my back I felt
his core hot and trembling through Kevlar.

Unteachable Moment

woe to the innocent who hears that sound!
—*Odyssey* 12.44, Fitzgerald translation

In lockdown, I'd been desperate
to hear sirens; once outside, safe,

they were too much. Paroxysmal,
dopplered, they blared past me *hur-ry*

hur-ry on the way to
my daughter's daycare,

and at home, in our living room, on the TV:
looped footage. Our near silence

punctured by the stifled lament
of police cars, ambulances careening to the ER,

converging on the scene
I'd just escaped.

My husband and I,
slumped on the couch,

unable to get out the oars, were watching
our daughter playing on the floor.

"That?" she asked, pointing
at the screen. "Ambulance," I said,

but she shook her head, still pointing,
her finger stirring the air.

I turned it right down but could still hear it.
I told her, "That's a *siren*,"

waited to see if she was satisfied
with just the word, or if she'd press me

for what the sound itself meant
this moment. I was queasy

watching my school on the news, as if learning
who and how many

could stanch the genre, as if the next
kept to himself wasn't also taking cues,

gearing up—shooting selfies, posed with his Glock—
and again, on every channel,

sirens will serenade kids filing from schools,
some with their arms on the shoulders of the kid ahead,

looking for all the world like anguished rowers.

I got down on the floor.

Now you can turn your personal gear into an on-the-go
bullet-proof shield

Order Kevlar packs
for the kids. If a shooter
comes you've got their back.

If

after James Hoch, Miscreants

if he had taken up guitar, played
ping-pong or Ultimate Frisbee, tried
deep breathing, accepted human frailty,
adopted a mutt at the SPCA,
shovelled his neighbour's walk,
did a year abroad
if there were more ways in than out
if he felt that someone was listening, maybe
a boy on the beach, after parasailing
at Île Sainte-Marguerite, the scent of umbrella pines
and eucalyptus in the air,
taking sips from a can of Kronenbourg
if his favourite aunt had been a police officer
if he'd had a favourite aunt
if his car had gotten a flat, and he'd taken this
as a sign to take a spiritual U-ie
if he had smelled fear and been able to name it,
if he could laugh at himself
if he'd read Dostoyevsky, Ian McEwan, Tim O'Brien
if he'd preferred the Guggenheim and techno gadgets to guns
if he made a mean gulab jamun or tiramisu or quindim
if it was so simple it was beautiful
if he'd had a sibling with cystic fibrosis, a teacher from Trinidad,
a chum who medalled in Taekwondo, a summer of love,
a walk in the park, a hug around the neck,
a Sudoku habit   if he had talked
to his doctor or mother and tried meds
and planted some sub-zero roses
if he had been pulled over for unpaid tickets,
bowed to cosmic irony and vowed to give peace

a chance   if he had not been born, or was somehow reborn
if we could recognize him this turn,
slip knot time, help him
to feel good in his skin
when he begins this
day and when he lays his head down to dream

Trigger Warning

The sun was shining outside
or it was raining. There were windows
but none of them opened.
I was wearing clothes but I was
naked, that first day back
in the classroom
after the shooting.
The next story we were
scheduled to read was
"The Things They Carried."
And when I stood before them and opened
my mouth I gave what was the first
trigger warning, before I knew
what such a thing was.
The story had guns and violence in it,
and I didn't know if they'd want
to read it now. Should we read it?
Or should we strike it?
No answer.
I asked again. Silence.
They were looking through me
as though I were the window and I was
looking at them like they were a door
with an unanswered phone ringing
behind it. They wouldn't
have names anymore because I was afraid
to love them. Finally, somebody
said, "We don't care." Nobody
disputed this. I was silent
for a long time.
Then I got my paper cup of coffee,

raised it to my mouth,
and poured it down the front of my blouse.

There is never just one trauma, the therapist says

Fired, fired, fired—that's why
I'm here. Months following the shooting
at my school, I fear I will be fired.
Never mind that my performance is good.
I've misfiled my students' names,
I float through the corridors
somewhere above my own jumpy prop.
As I run for the bus I envision my house swallowed by fire.
Hats off to the mind's gymnastics,
how it can juggle and riddle and pun
so that the discharging of the gun, the firearm
firing now months later activates a fear in me
to be fired, which is really fallout—cue to
my big childhood trauma: the torching of our house
by our tenant, at night while we slept.
Doctor moves a pencil back and forth
like the pendulum of a metronome
and my gaze follows it, *tick tock, tick tock,*
redirecting eye movements as I revisit
one of the doppelgänger traumas, to re-process it.
You, too, can try this at home, by pressing the top of each knee
like a cat kneading a cushion before a nap
you, too, can try this at home, pressing the top of each knee
one of the doppelgänger traumas, to re-process it,
redirecting eye movements. As I revisit
and my gaze follows it, *tick tock, tick tock,*
like the pendulum of a metronome,
Doctor moves a pencil back and forth
by our tenant, at night while we slept.
My big childhood trauma: the torching of our house,
to be fired, which is really fallout—cue to
firing now months later activates a fear in me

so that the discharging of the gun, the firearm—
how it can juggle and riddle and pun—
hats off to the mind's gymnastics!
As I run for the bus I envision my house swallowed by fire.
Somewhere above my own jumpy prop
I float through the corridors.
I've misfired my students' names.
Never mind that my performance is good,
at my school, I fear I will be fired.
I'm here. Months following the shooting
fired, fired, fired—that's why!

Teaching Philosophy, Revised

After the shooting at my school (which was sometime after
and sometime before shootings at other schools),

I'd observe my students as they abstained from taking notes,
slogged through an exam, or zoned out

while I soft-shoed my way through tropes and figures.
I began to see them

as perhaps the flight attendant, during the performance
of the in-flight safety monologue, regards the suits

reading papers, row upon row of heads
hooked up to gadgets. And, lighting on

one face,
on an exhale,

I'd say to myself, *This is somebody's child.*

Nostalgic for the speedbird rigour
that fuelled my early years of teaching,

now I also reckon its cost
in missed connections, in the time lost

composing my final comments on papers
not collected, stowed in file drawers

where my mantra, *Be
as precise as possible, whenever possible,*

fades away like contrails in the ether.

I think, *If I teach nothing else today,*
let me show compassion to somebody's child.

And, in case poetry may save as many lives
as floor-level lighting and safety hatches,

let me be as philosophical as the flight attendant,
my near double in the sister city of work,

as I cope with constraints of space and time,
in a milieu fraught with risk, attending

to the needs of people who want
to get somewhere else

yet might still enjoy the flight.

In Retrospect

> *and then it was over, / and then it had just begun.*
> —Bob Hicok, "In the Loop"

"Eight years on, I can't look at his photograph
or even say his name," says one of my colleagues.
I *need* to look
though it does no good.

The only rhymes for people
are *steeple, needle, seagull*—
miscellaneous wrenched, off,
and broken rhymes. *Peep hole.*

I bought a laser-beam key chain
to pinpoint words on the screen.
Sorting and ranking are the compulsive
hand washing of the news cycle.
The worst mass shooting in history,
a veiled challenge to outdo.

Then there's *active shooter.*
Too athletic, smacks of retail:
                    Active Shooter,
          for all your active shooting needs.
          This month, 10% off ammo.

It's not complete without a Forensic Biography
segment: the signs, in hindsight.

Two weeks or so before it happened,
I looked up the extension for Security,
thinking someone could walk in here with a gun,

like they did at the Polytechnique,
and at Concordia, and at the high school in my home town,
when I was seven and hadn't ever considered
that a guitar case could be used
to carry anything but a guitar.

Conventions

> *the same message: how horrible it was, how little*
> *there was to say about how horrible it was.*
> —Bob Hicok, "In the Loop"

The running and then
the footage of people running.
After the chaos there is silence,
a failure of words but not of sound,
which we know travels in waves,
and the speed of which is still the distance
travelled per unit of time.
The sound of a firearm going off
in a school hallway is not unlike the sound
of a metal locker slamming inside your head.
The colleagues you hugged
and who hugged you will go back
to arms' length, which is healthy.
Maybe you will cry
one night doing dishes,
up to the elbow in thinning suds,
combing for straggling flatware,
which might suggest something poetic
about the correspondence of the elements
or, when you think about it, the extraordinary
capacity of the workaday to anchor
and unmoor us.

Blooms for Anastasia

Anastasia—Latinized and feminized form of the Greek Αναστασιος (Anastasios) which means "resurrection" from Greek αναστασις (anastasis) (composed of the elements ανα (ana) "up" and στασις (stasis) "standing").

Amaryllis, Buttercup, Cosmos, Daisy,
Edelweiss, Freesia, Gladiola, Hydrangea,
Iris, Jonquil, Kangaroo Paw, Larkspur,
Monkshood, Narcissus, Orchid, Peony,
Queen Anne's Lace, Rose, Sunflower, Tulip,
Ursinia, Veronica, Wildflowers,
Xeranthemum, Yarrow, Zinnia.

Not enough. Words. Flowers.
In every way insufficient. But I can't not
name you, when we remember the name
of the shooter, shooters, of the schools
where shootings took place.
                                        Took
place. I want to say that they did not
take place. We who survived reclaimed
our places, patched the walls,
planted a peace garden—a gesture
better than my catalogue of blooms
because your family can sit in that garden,
where the bulbs your friends planted pulse
to life, and the sun shines and the rain falls.

Child/not-child whose name is a perennial

in the atrium of our school—
Wrong not to name you,

and to have to name you.

The Worst

Then was all care at an end, and they lived in great joy together.
—The Brothers Grimm

What you thought you couldn't endure
you lived through and something else
became the worst—all at once
or in increments. The worst telescopes,
may be happiest in the future, barely
detectable, like a shadow on the lung
below the whorl and grain of ultrasound.

We learn that hubris connects Sisyphus and schlep.
In Greek mythology we say *nemesis*.
In therapy we say *lifestyle* and *rock bottom*.
An anagram for *ruined* is *inured*.
The waxed doorknobs of semantics!

How do we get a handle on the worst
when it's a moving target, always beyond
the baldly conceivable and
unimaginable—beyond lynchings
and postcards of lynchings?
It must be that there are more worsts
than ways to parse them:
the personal and the collective, the local
and the global, and the worst is where
they overlap. I think of that
bus in New Delhi and can't think.
What pill blurs the mismatch
between our need for meaning
and our inability to find it?

When what feels like the worst happens
to us, I wish us an eye
of oblivion that we can enter
like a licked thread,
and somebody ties the knot.

A pendulum swinging to and fro
between boredom and pain,
is what Schopenhauer thought.

What if the worst,
rather than always receding
like the mirage of water on the road ahead,
is more like a threshold
so what we thought was the worst is
only an opening?

Threshold

Event Horizon

Getting closer to the due date,
I feared going out alone, unable to
utter my darkest thought: someone could
slice open my belly and steal my baby.
Trudging to the pharmacy,
I'd envision the car stopping beside me,
the hand forcing my head, cop-show-style,
into the back seat where everything
fades to black.

And then, before my baby was two months old, it happened
to someone in Missouri, in her own home.
And it wasn't my slaver or pedophile,
but a woman my age
whose ex had just filed for custody of their kids.

How did she get past the door?
Was it in broad daylight? Can a horror
enter the world when you break the seal
on a thought? Am I ready
to chuck the fallacy of false cause
along with the paper?

What, exactly, is
unthinkable?

There is a hazy, unnameable
genre I'd shunt beyond the event horizon
if I could. O self-
swallowing spirit of thresholds,

undo the birth

of fears that can't be scattered,
like roaches in a dark kitchen,
by flicking on the lights.

In Praise of Hospital Cafeterias

Water, is taught by thirst.
—Emily Dickinson

Not exactly an oasis in the desert,
but as you bide time before the biopsy
or loosen your watch to let the news
sink in, good to avail yourself
of the $2.22 coffee & muffin combo
or Fairlee pulp-free OJ & bagel,
benign beige plastic chair,
dusty plant languishing on a ledge:
a single bloom, reaching
toward the window's frosted glass.
On another day this plant
would be giving God the finger.
The food service worker's skirt
argues with her butt. Luck
sounds like a word a baby might say,
trying out her tongue. So what
if you have forgotten the common names
of trees, the taste of a carrot with the dirt
just rubbed off, which bird
says *youcheeseburger, cheeseburger,*
cheeseburger, cheeseburg.
There is ordinary comfort in wrapped straws.
A lady is scraping a muffin paper
with her teeth, so
beautiful. For now
there is no bloom of blood in the syringe—
magenta, a magician's scarf.
Here you are:

a hiatus before climbing an endless flight
of unpainted stairs or sitting at home, suffering
the Muzak of the incontinent faucet.

Adventures in Microgravity

After my sister's second round of chemo
we take the baby to visit. I hover,
try on her wigs, stir fry kale with garlic
while she's anchored in bed with two cats and a dog,
the arm with the cannula draped over a pillow
like an expensive watch.

To my daughter she's no different
than the day they first locked eyes,
short months ago. My sister cradled her
football-style for her first bath, showed us
how to swab her cord.

Nurse-maid, she checked the stitches of my tear,
warned me not to look.
Shopped, cooked a Thanksgiving turkey,
soothed the baby while I filled my second plate.
Dishes, the kitchen floor, you name it.
All the while she was on tenterhooks,
dodging her doctor's call, keeping mum.

For months, each of us has drifted
alone in her fear. Tomorrow
we will drive to the city, wait together
in a small pink office at Sunnybrook.

From outer space we might be seen
orbiting the two women
sitting on stolid chairs below us.
They fill out forms. Each blunt
thought is like a book falling off a ladder.

One grasps the other's hand
as the oncologist assesses her suitability for radiation.
The other's breasts harden with milk.

Nightmare

There's a woman smacking a toddler,
the contact of palm on bare skin, the cries
as she staples her hand to his back
like someone upholstering a chair.
One of those four-story brick apartment houses
the colour of bread crust—aluminum doors,
concrete balconies clogged with baby gear, hibachis.
Four stories up: the woman on her back, moored
to the concrete, the blond-haired boy—in just a diaper—
draped across her chest. He's cried out now.
And now she's not moving, he crawls across her
and sticks his head through the balcony's metal bars—
they can't be wide enough for him but they are; shoulders
so narrow he squeezes through as though being born.

Strict Bed Rest

PPROM: Preterm Premature Rupture of Membranes (the amniotic sac is ruptured, resulting in leakage of amniotic fluid. It is considered "preterm" when it occurs before 37 weeks).

The mind can only do so much knitting.
Rounds of TV, novels, magazines, surfing the web
between three squares and rest might sound good, but
PPROM means no dancing.

TV's scary, WebMD says odds aren't good.
Novels make me cry, even Jane Austen.
"PPROM means we dance after twenty-eight weeks?"
My doctor's reply is open-ended,

makes me cry. No escape in Jane Austen.
"My Department Chair asked when I'm coming back."
My doctor's reply is open-ended:
"We're amazed you're still carrying this baby!"

"Are you coming back?" my Department Chair asks.
"Only if my ship sinks," I want to say.
If I lose the baby before twenty weeks
I'll come back. After twenty it's full leave

even if my ship sinks. Nobody knows
what to expect, nobody knows when
I'll come back. After twenty it's full leave.
I only get up to pee. Sisters cook.

Nobody knows what to expect when
odds aren't good. They crown me PPROM Queen,
let me get up to pee. My sisters cook.
At twenty-eight weeks they bring me cake, gifts

because our good vessel's still sea-worthy.
We spend my fortieth birthday in bed.
Every week after week twenty-eight: cake, gifts.
Through glass I watch bare branches parry wind.

We spend Hubby's birthday in bed too. He broke
his leg carrying our daughter uphill.
Through glass I watch trees bud, buds split.
This goes on forever. Baby's due in June.

My sisters carry all of us uphill.
I'm afraid to love and lose my baby.
This goes on forever. He's due late June.
The ultrasound image is my dark map.

I tell him I love him, say *keep growing*.
It's not a train, Sylvia Plath; it's a raft.
The ultrasound image is my dark map.
His constellation lights up the night sky.

It's a raft there's no getting off. Others
bring me provisions, offer distractions.
His constellation lights up the night sky.
I drift, notch the days on my soft body.

Provisions, distractions,
three squares, hope. I rest and I'm restless.
I drift, notch the days on my soft body,
which (*how?*) persists in its sublime knitting.

Fury to Bed Rest

> Navigare necesse est vivere non est necesse. *(To sail is necessary; to live is not necessary.)*
> —Attributed by Plutarch to Gnaeus Pompeius Magnus

Everything at one remove—
someone coughing in another room,
a painting of a ship on a roiling sea,
a bad painting, hung askew.

A Buddhist said worry is an act
of violence, to be anywhere
other than the present moment,
violence.
           Release regret,
release fear of loss, or I might lose
my waters, the sea cyclone
down the drain, the tub's
black umbilicus.

Release. I weigh light, sew shut
windows at night, sleep, half-sleep
under a starless sky. Release.

A nurse says, "We'd hang you
upside down if we could." I lie still,
pillows under my knees.

In the drain a blinking fish eye.

Whole hours I'm paralyzed with fear,
unable to pick up the phone, or switch off
the light, or roll over, or sob.

Gift Horse

No old-time bonnets with eyelet trim;
this baby wasn't born yesteryear.
No plastic shoes. We eschew

things that scratch, bind, itch.
Ditto Velcro and rompers with
buttons up the back, sans front closures.

Please, nothing with cutesy
embroidered pseudo-French expressions
or amicable-looking snails

slithering amongst pastel-toned garden tools.
Nothing advertising an institution.
No fossil-fuel-eating-vehicle motifs.

Anything laden with thwarted dreams
however bright, however lovely,
will be promptly set free to the Goodwill.

No mohair shrugs, pleather
skorts, animal prints,
rhinestones, fun-fur, pinstripes, no hint

of a life wasted or scripted.
Nothing too girl, nothing too boy.
Nothing redolent of upper crust.

Nothing sad, ugly, tired, prone to stain.
Nothing that reminds us of pain.

New Father's Guidebook, A–Z

All babies cry, Daddy-O.
Every father, guaranteed,
holds inside joy's key.
Love makes noise.

Over pitifully quick.
Remember silence,
the ultimate valium,
when _____ Xs your Zzzzs.

My Daughter, Crying Herself to Sleep

Crying herself to sleep, my daughter
has turned her back on me. Even

the soles of her feet shrink from my touch.
Before her first steps they were softer

than my wrists. Now I think of the skin
on a pudding brought to the boil

and left to simmer. She has a temper,
she's being weaned. Not enough milk

since I went back to work. Sobs
regular as purl stitches, her rage winds down

in lurches. She's turned away from me,
curled into herself, tetchy and aloof.

Pushed off, in open water.
My little cutter's going to sail the world.

I wanted to watch my own caesarean and see you born

The surgeon grunted behind the drape.
You were planted on my chest for one minute.
Then they repacked me like a bento box,
double stitched, and I was sent to Recovery,
where I had to prove I could move my legs
before I could hold you again;
I was swimming to you under taut sheets.

Now there have been days
I've had to hold you down for a needle,
for electrodes, for a sub-dermal needle stim-probe,
as you fought and called out, "Mama, help me!"
and I was half-elated you were stringing words together.

Listen to me, when there are no words
I will feel the ribs of the animal, I will
devise the way out.
Hold me to it.

Threshold

It took two nurses and your dad to hold you
down for the IV. The nurse with the needle
plunged for a vein, which you'd scuppered
in your rage. First one fist, then the other,
your turbo-cry shredding the scenery,
and that one marathon howl—nothing
can ever be academic for me now,
at your feet. Nor for your dad, the heavy,
who'll carry you into the Farraday cage,
catch your head when the Nembutal drops
anchor, lay you down like a wilted bouquet
on the MRI bed. He'll sit vigil
while you're in the whale's gut, under a striped
flannel. Double earplugs, pacifier:
your protection from the runway din
of magnets doing the bump, this sunless spell.

From behind the observation glass, I
let you go, too. Burlap and twine swaddle
the shrub in winter. The word *dolor*.
In my mind's vault, I still hold you—
we rise with each swell, dip
with each trough, look
to the far shore.

Ativan

Fleck of wherewithal. Just
to have it in a tiny faux-
abalone box, to know you can
lift it with a licked pinkie,
if required. Bitter
plaster-of-Paris smear
under the tongue
                    because
the mind's default is flee
and your baby's lumbar puncture
is scheduled for 2:30. Necessity
and consent
in a slow dissolve.
Not so much a buffer
as the strength to stand
beside the hospital bed
and be two of the hands
holding him for the needle's kiss.

Descent

My baby was still nursing, and I'd lean over
the bed's steel rails to give him the breast,
let him twist his fingers in my hair until he slept
anchored by electrodes, gauze bonnet, fat snarl of wires
twisting into a Bob the Builder backpack
that housed the Trackit box near the call switch.
I could not leave the ward though they urged me to
go home, get a shower, change. At night,
an infrared video camera captured our quiet ballet.

I could not leave, could not leave. On the third day
I was sent down to the basement,
to the abandoned locker room.
Past the heavy steel door that would not quite close,
I stood under exposed ducts, frazzled fluorescent tubes
in a ship's bilge. Whiff of mildew, occult drip.
In the dim light I found the one narrow
shower stall, the slick edge
of the torn plastic curtain, pulled it back.

No one to hear me. My baby
lay in a bed flights up, electrodes
pasted to his scalp, helmeted in gauze.
I stripped, hung my milk-sour track suit
and hospital towel on a hook, stepped over the lip
onto a flattened shopping bag spread like a lily pad
on the blackened grout, institutional-green tiles.
The first cold water,
my baptism.

Miracle

Walled in by Plexiglas, we warmed vinyl
until the intercom garbled our son's name.
The door hummed like a grade-school teacher
with a pitch pipe, and we pushed through
into a white hallway lined with close-ups of daisies.
The psychologist had an accent, East Clinical
or Impending Retirement, I couldn't quite place it.
She asked our two-year-old to push a toy stroller
to her door. Things went downhill from there:
he dropped toys, wouldn't pick them up.
                                          "You must
make him," she insisted, "use hand-over-hand technique."
We can't tell if he's willful or if our bidding
to him is as the wind to the ocean floor.
                                          "It's not okay
to cross the street after the signal.
Someone says *goodbye*, it's the time to reply,
not long after," she averred. The long-after
poet in me hugged the mother in me, deflated
by the psychologist's prediction
of assisted living.
                    "You look sad,"
she said, less observation
than sugared jeer. "No," I said,
swiping the emoticon for *sandbagged* from my face.
I reached for the Disability Tax Credit forms
she held out like cocktail napkins.
My husband said, "What I hope for him
is that he'll be able to have a relationship, connect
with someone."
She had the look of a croupier
raking in chips for the house.

                    "Barring a miracle,"
said the psychologist, "he'll be a good candidate
for a special needs school."

"You a psychologist or a psychic?" Long after,
in this poem, I can say that.
In her office, though, beyond Plexiglas
and the mandatory umbrella-check,
I said goodbye, ran
to my afternoon class,
arriving dazed, rain-splattered, in my coat,
to teach the assigned poem,
"Pied Beauty." Reading Hopkins aloud
to fresh, unworldly faces,
this time,
when I got to *All things counter,*
original, spare, strange, the skin of my life
caught in the teeth of the poem
and it sang through me.

After the diagnosis I went to the pool to ease into cold fact

for Wes

Tell me joy persists. I need that to hold
as I parse the lengthening shadows:
therapies, special schools, the thinning hope
that he may speak, ride a bike, beat the odds.

You were back at home, resting with our son.
And just when I should have been packing up,
I caught sight of a Chinese kite, a dragon,
red, swooping in the wind and so high up

I thought it must have broken free, lost.
"Look, someone's kite escaped!" a boy exclaimed,
pointing skyward. There the kite danced, wind-tossed,
too high to think it held by any hand.

Yet, buoyed, I watched it for a good long time,
until I felt the nature of the rhyme.

Broken Baby Blues

Can I say it to myself, I've got the broken baby blues?
Can I say it to the wind, I've got the broken baby blues?
Listen to me sister, walk a mile in my shoes.

My baby's perfect but his brain won't let him talk.
Said my baby's perfect but his brain won't let him talk.
A doctor helped my baby learn to walk.

I feared before his birth that something might go wrong.
When we stitched him in the womb I feared something might go
    wrong.
Now I fear for myself because I'm singing this song.

I love my sweet baby and I want to do him right.
Yes, I love my sweet baby and I aim to do him right.
Don't know how to mend his ills—I'm living darkest night.

Ain't no mama nowhere safe from broken baby blues.
No daddy—God in heaven!—hasn't paid his dues.
Lord God save my baby from the broken mama blues.

Happy Blues

*A "blue note" is a note from outside of a given tonality which gives
that tonality (or chord, etc.) a dissonant "bite." Most blue notes
come from the vocal practice (later imitated by horn players and
guitarists) of "sliding" into notes from either a half step above or
below rather than landing right on them, which produces a "dirty" or
"bluesy" sound which most often resolves to the "correct" note from
within the tonality.*
—Durrlman Hesse

We want to leave you happy, / Don't want to leave you sad.
—Ella Fitzgerald

It hits me: there should be video of my son while he's not having a
seizure or collapsing, marionette-like, in episodic ataxia. Something
not for the doctors but for us, something that, when we watch it
months later, elicits a comparatively uncomplicated joy.

Dues, one and two
Dues, doesn't matter nothing

So this time, I film him while he's playing, sure of his grip on the
disk-shaped beads, which he stacks on pegs set into a wooden base,
following what must be his own sense of order. He's four, atypical.
His sense of order is beads jumbled, mouthed, dropped on the floor.

Dues, three and four
Dues, maybe more, that's all right

I film him as he says, "on, om, on on," and slides beads onto a peg.
On the tallest peg he slides two red pentagons, a green circle, fol-
lowed by two more reds, capped by a blue square. Then he turns it

upside down to begin again. Now blue first on the red peg. Then he brings the toy to his mouth as though taking a sip from red's blue spout.

I've sung these blues, and I'm through
Cause I don't know what I'm singing about

Look, he's put four red pentagons together—capped by a green circle on the red peg. Albers' colour studies dance in my mind's eye. I film for 34 seconds and have to stop to pick up the blue bead that fell when he mouthed the toy. He'd leaned over the side of his trip-trap chair, reaching for blue, saying "Help me, help me." "Get it?" I asked. And he looked at me, repeated, "Geddee," happy to be understood.

I am happy you are happy too
I am happy you are happy too

Watching and re-watching our video together, we're transfixed. He glances down at his chest, tugs at his Gap t-shirt, recognizing it from the clip. Every time we hear the bead drop in our recorded scene, in reply to my line, "Get it?" he answers again, out loud, "Geddee," in sync with the boy in the video grasping the toy, looking at the floor and then over at his mom, who replies, "I'll get it, hold on."

So let's go out with the blues that's swinging
Like Count Basie, swing on
Like Count Basie, swing on
Like Count Basie, swing on
Like Count Basie, swing on
Swing on, swing out tonight

Going Under

It goes too fast: lighting the first candle,
packing the painting smock in the entry-level backpack
the first day of kindergarten. Feed him with a spoon.
Carry her up to bed after a day at the beach.
Nostalgia is the pain of going home and the pain

of not being able to go home.
At seventy-three, my friend Vi says, "I'd have another if I could."
She had six babies, gave them tea in a bottle,
aired them in their pram on the balcony in March,
starched all their little white dresses, and
offers me, without irony, this consolation: "You get to
have him as a baby a while longer." I appreciate
its truth and its sting (in the same way
I appreciate the thought that at least
Marilyn Monroe died when she was still beautiful).

I nuzzle my son's damp hair as he sleeps on the sofa.
He tangles his fingers in my hair, insisting
even in sleep on my constant presence.
Infant, from the Latin for *unable to speak*.
At five and nonverbal, our boy's still golden.
People like to say *No one goes to college in diapers.*

I find it easiest when we're at home.
When we mingle with children his age and their parents,
he bears the sigil of his delays. He hugs strangers.
He still eats sand. He wields an ear-piercing scream.
He develops, but the gap widens
like the distance between two swimmers
when one is caught in a rip current.

In my dream I shout *Swim parallel to the shore!*
my voice lost in the crashing surf.
Seaweed clutches at my ankles
as I plunge into the murk.
We are both struggling.
Onlookers struggle to help,
or to brave helplessness.

Watch him save us I say, going under.

First Outing with Adaptive Stroller

Then the eyes of both of them were opened
—Genesis 3:7

I didn't see them before, those parents
pushing a small-scale wheelchair down narrow
aisles at the grocery store. But I know
I must have yielded way, conveyed the pleasant
stranger vibe, appeared—if they saw me—decent,
a patient smile waiting to reach for Brasso
or Bounce—back when I bought Bounce and Brasso
and Endust—exalting things convenient.

I hardly saw the child. It's not polite
to stare, but that's not why. If I knew how
to pry off blinders and dwell in insight,
would I self-inflict it? It happens now
a taste for irony is our birthright:
we learn to love by the sweat of our brow.

At the Ophthalmologist's

The doctor will use a few eye drops to help your child's pupils dilate, creating a better window to the back of your child's eyes.

Our son doesn't like this very much.
My husband has to sit in the examination chair
and restrain him for the drops.

The drops take about 45 minutes to work, will blur your child's vision and cause a little light sensitivity for a few hours.

Waiting room is to day as month is to year.

When the drops have supersized the pupils,
we are called from the waiting room
back into the dimly-lit exam room
with its peeling cartoon decals.

Using a retinoscope, the doctor will move the light to see it reflected in the pupil.

Our son doesn't like this very much.
My husband has to sit in the examination chair
and restrain him.

A normal cornea is round like a baseball. With astigmatism, the cornea curves more severely, like a football.

Vending machine is to meltdown as Band-Aid is to whiplash.

But how well can our son see? we ask.
I don't have an answer for that, he says.
As long as our son is nonverbal,

we can never know for sure.
Depth perception is an open question.

A script for spectacles,
a recommended optometrist.

Packing up, small talk.
The doctor learns we're doctors, too—though not the "real" kind:
my husband teaches Shakespeare;
I like to use this as an example of metonymy.

Then the ophthalmologist gets a turn. He asks
whether *Hamlet* was written before the Reformation.
"Was Shakespeare Catholic?" he wants to know.
I can see how this might be an important question.
"Which Reformation?" my husband asks.
He tries to give the ophthalmologist a good answer,
but things with Shakespeare are complicated.

That's how we leave it.
Answer is to question as window is to clock.

Grammar of a Sleep Disorder

Our son has been pole-vaulting from sleep
at 1 or 2 a.m. We are the sand pit.
We take shifts until the melatonin strip
parleys with the neurons.
If that's a bust, a pill cutter
halves a Trazodone. Time
in the middle of the night
moves as slowly as the gerund in a poem.
We are not grateful for it.
It's not like you're going fishing,
ticking off 12 Things
Successful People Do Before Breakfast.
We've tried the typical remedies;
typically, they have not worked.
Warm milk! A drive to the West Island!
Imperative: sleep,
cut out for a few minutes
before the day full-throttle
rebegins—the little propellers
of his hands limp and heavy, snagged
in my knotted hair,
drifting towards the falls.
What's round and full as the moon?
A joke without a punchline.

For Magnus, at Seven

In one of my alternating off-hours

while your Dad took his turn sitting up

with unsleeping you—

dragonfly

caught in the badminton net—

I dreamed

tick tock   you'd grown up,

and now you stood,

yourself and not yourself,

wearing a muted suit and lace-up shoes.

You sunk into a wicker chair, which creaked

when you picked up one foot as I kneeled down

to untie.

You accidentally kicked me

in the eye, as you often do—

gross-motor glitch

which made the dream seem *real,*

a sort of proof.

I took your shoes off and then your socks, so

many pairs one on top of the other

and all full of holes—

not like real life,

where I dress you well and never narrate to you

my dreams—layer after layer

socks, socks, socks   I pulled until, at last

your feet—

bean-bag fat and small as a toddler's,

like fleshy little doorstops in my cupped hands—were

a silent fact,

an emblem

between us in the dark.

After Meeting with the School Psychologist

If I wasn't going to be that lady crying in the train,
I needed to drive a wedge between my throat
and the boxes in the latest psych report showing
Adaptive Level and *Age Equivalent in Four Key Domains.*

I'd brought the new issue of *House Beautiful*
and, the entire ride home, I anchored myself
to that shelter mag. I needed slick copy, captions,
flooring ads as a point of focus, a steadying blur.

June's issue vaunts the colour yellow: *Pure colors*
speak a language all their own, without screaming at you;
Not your typical primary or buttery yellow—
like happily lounging inside a buttercup.

I flipped smooth pages, making that little snap,
to hold at bay the words *assessments converge*
to support a diagnosis of severe intellectual disability.
I willed ice in the veins. *Bourgeois Bitch,*

the girls in Doc Martens no doubt dubbed me, reading like a
bird pecking seeds in traffic: peck, jump, peck,
swoop, peck—hardscrabble, avoiding
the gravel of the phrase *global development quotient.*

I climbed the métro stairs, spurring myself:
don't cry, swallow it, swallow.
June's all about the colour yellow.
My son's room is Limesicle, Benjamin Moore.

To his light fixture I taped a map of the world.
It illuminates pastel continents, blue-green seas.
You get an impression of old-timey expeditions: dogsleds,
a ship beset, covered in rime near the North pole.

With a magnifying glass, you can read tiny script:
Highest point reached by man, Greely Expedition 1881.

I gripped the railing the whole way up the two flights
to ground level, tethered to the question *What's Modern Now?*

Quick

"That's enough! How can you let him get away with that?"
I hear a woman shout at my husband near the Pik-Nik.
Our son has screamed one too many times,
band-saw-on-steel-pipe screams. Who hasn't heard
such a child? From the shoe store, where I've the cushier job
of helping our daughter pick out sneakers, I heard him,
thrashing in my husband's grasp, stomping, going Jell-O
trying to break free, to hurtle through the mall.

                              He's five.
For him, words are balloons that have floated away.
Running came late and he wants to keep it.

"I'm sorry ma'am, he may not look like it,
but this is a special-needs child," my husband says,
in a tone I would call even, if I didn't know better.
There's no adjective for this inflection. Call it
river otter versus crocodile. One of many
leaves falling from the oak.
                        The Chinese word *Téng*—
to love—said by a parent to a child
uses the same character as *to hurt*.

From the store's entrance, I can see the woman
and her burly partner dry-erase the air
around their fast-food trays. "Sorry, never mind,"
they both say, as though they'd tried to order breakfast
after the lunch menu went up.

I drift back to my daughter, who's sinking
in a quicksand of shoes.

We reunite with the boys,
drop some loonies into mechanical ponies.
Cross the parking lot together.
"The cashier at the wine store said, 'Some people
are such jerks,'" my husband offers, quietly,
hands square on the wheel, and it is consoling.

Are thicker skins on sale at Reitman's?
Will I shop online?
A glass of wine might not be enough
for me, the brooder who'll replay, replay, replay
the rebuke ricocheted around the mall,
hovering its mirror inches from everyone's nose. Cut
to my son who has to hear
his father offer this defense to a stranger.
The unnameable tone.

Tone comes from the Greek for *to stretch*—
a reaching towards or a pulling away.
Shouldn't we be used to it by now?

'...a phenomenon called wave setup...happens when a wave breaks and doesn't have time to fully recede before another wave breaks and runs up on top of it.' ...On an otherwise nice beach weather day, these swells can be deadly.

— hurricane specialist Michael Lowry, quoted in "Maui Beach Flooded by Waves Generated by a Storm 5,000 Miles Away," Jon Erdman, weather.com

Within a half hour of arriving on Maui, we're at Napili beach. A quick walk to shake off two days of travel, cancelled and delayed flights, airport limbo. *Travel* comes from *travail*. All that falls away as we kick off our flip-flops. I hold my son by the hand and he bounds into the water up to his knees, back out, then back in—his obsession with thresholds rewarded here—and for a moment we're both typical, giddy. "Careful," my husband says over his shoulder, walking along the sand with our daughter and his mom. Our son, unwary, is his own universe. The bottoms of my beach pants are barely wet. Back out, then back in.

When we're hit by the first wave, my hand slips from his. I lunge forward to grab him but with my left hand I only catch a bit of his UV-rash-guard shirt, between the shoulder blades, my fingers clamping down like the jaws of a she-wolf on her pup when she needs to move him, quick. The backwash so strong it pulls my feet out from under me as I scramble backwards, tugging, gripping that fistful of rash guard, trying to keep his head above water and get out.

A second, bigger, wave and I go under too—my head hits bottom. When I try to come up, a third wave. Mouth, nose and ears fill with sand as we're pulled out fast by the undertow. That bit of rash guard, bright white—just my fingers now. Can't think, can't shout for help, every cell thrumming: *don't let go, don't let go.*

Then a hand grabbing *me* by the shirt and pulling me out and me pulling my son by a pinch of rash guard. Sputtering and coughing sand, more sand, sand. I hear the man say he'd never seen that much sand come out of anyone. "You got pasted!" Clothes sandbag-heavy and full. Grit in my throat, roar in my ears. Under an outdoor shower for ten minutes, I sway, rubbing off and spitting out sand. Our daughter slouches on a bench while my husband and mother-in-law tend to our little boy, who is agitated but not crying. Fearless, he'd go back in.

What must be turned, turned in the palm like a stone picked up at the beach? That night I bolt upright from sleep, sweat breaking on my skin, roar of the sea in my ears. Not 5000 miles away, but here: my churning terror. I might have let go.

I might have let go.

Alive

A flame we have tended,
cupping our hands around him,
our backs to the wind.

From the earliest days
EEG showed abnormal activity.
Misfiring neurons. Meds

tamped the seizures
so that he might advance,
reach milestones.

Some milestones he has met.
Others tumbled as scree
down a steep slope.

We say *We love you!*
You are strong!
Leap up!

And when he leaps
we say *bravo*! Or *danger*!
because he knows no fear

will not hear *no*,
does not sleep, driven
to pull the tree down,

smash mirrors, family photos,
swallow the glass, everything
in his mouth. Your hair,

my arm. Seven years on
and we tend, turning
our frazzled hours to his needs

and sleeping, when permitted,
like logs, like dried timber.
He gets stronger. See

how he licks the walls,
turns direction unpredictably
on the stairs. We tend this blaze,

every day,
every day willing
to be burned. Every day

alive.

Grass

> *O I perceive after all so many uttering tongues!*
> —Walt Whitman, "A child said, What is the grass?"

"Grass," I said, plopping down in the park.
"Grass," Magnus said,
squatting to pat it with his palms.
He was two.
Since then, four seasons of grass, fresh cut,
browning and strewn with leaves, have passed.
Grass was a one-time word, one of many
one-time words that grew and were mown,
scattered to the wind. Yet we held it once—
damp and green and ordinary.

Museum of Kindness

My First Daughter

Joe Kennedy Sr.

That's my first daughter sitting behind me,
looking as happy as the rest. Rosemary.
Unlike the others. Slower to roll, crawl,
talk. An army of tutors taught her all
she knew of reading, writing, maths and such;
she didn't shine at school or home. Too much
for her—fourth grade math and fifth grade English
her limit. Eunice, wanting to distinguish
Rosemary, pronounced her "best teeth and smile."
She was beautiful, could pass for normal.
Kids included her as crew when they'd compete,
though she couldn't row or cut her own meat
or hold her own at the dinner table.
In '39 it was still bearable.
I wish you'd bring it here, so I can see it.
Since the stroke, just thoughts. If I could say it...
That one was shot at Eden-Roc, Antibes,
a little paradise. In May the debs
wore Molyneux gowns to dine with the King
and Queen. A month in Eden-Roc, last fling
before the war. We're holding the gold here,
each of us bathed in slanting light before
the shit hits the fan. Joe Jr. and Jack
over from Harvard. The whole clan, before Kick
gave her hand to an Anglican—yes, that
worked Rose up quite a bit. Right off the bat
I wrote to Kick, *You are still and always*
will be tops with me. The truth is, it pays
to be a winner and Kick won: her catch

was heir to the Duke of Devonshire. *Match
point*, I thought. If you want to make money,
go where the money is. Turned out a sorry
business, though: her Billy dead before
he inherited the dukedom and sired an heir,
and then to lose our best girl Kick, too, so
soon after the bloody war took Joe. Joe.
And now I've watched Jack and Bobby cut down
on TV. Every time I turn around:
death. And me in a crank bed having my
ass wiped. Pull my gown down in the back, try
to put yourself in my place. I thought it
would help—the procedure. She was out
of control, escaping at night, coming
home with leaves in her hair. Becoming
a woman. Getting fat. Rose would've died.
Joe Jr. wouldn't've had a chance. We'd tried
everything. Freeman and Watts had success
with others. With Rosemary they messed up
royally. For seven years we kept her
at Craig House, then we put her in the care
of the nuns at St. Coletta's, Wisconsin.
I couldn't visit. Of course the children
knew it was forbidden to ask. You learn
what rules to break. I've never talked, I earned
so they could serve and attain eminence.
If Eunice had balls she'd be President.

Charles Darwin on His Namesake, Charles Waring Darwin

a found poem

Our poor baby was born December 6th, 1856
and died on June 28th, 1858. He was small
for his age and backward in walking and talking, but intelligent
and observant. When crawling naked on the floor he looked

very elegant. He had never been ill and cried less than any
of our babies. He was of a remarkably sweet, placid
and joyful disposition; but had not high spirits, and
did not laugh much. He often made strange grimaces and shivered,

when excited; but did so also, for a joke
and his little eyes used to glisten, after pouting or stretching
widely his little lips. He used sometimes to move his mouth as if
talking loudly, but making no noise, and this he did when very

happy. He was particularly fond of standing on my hands
and being tossed in the air; and then he always smiled, and made
a little pleased noise. I had just taught him to kiss me.
He would lie for a long time placidly on my lap looking

with a steady and pleased expression at my face; sometimes trying
to poke his little fingers into my mouth, or making nice
little bubbling noises as I moved his chin. I had taught him
not to scratch, but when I said, "Giddlums never scratches now"

he could not always resist a little grab, and then he would
look at me with a wicked little smile. He would play for any
length of time on the sofa, letting himself fall suddenly,
and looking over his shoulder to see that I was ready.

He was very affectionate and had a passion for Parslow
and it was very pretty to see his extreme eagerness
with outstretched arms, to get to him. Our poor little
darling's short life has been placid, innocent

and joyful. I think and trust he did not suffer so much
at last, as he appeared to do; but the last 36 hours
were miserable beyond expression.
In the sleep of Death he resumed his placid looks.

Mark Twain, December 25, 1909, on the Death of His
Daughter Jean, Who Drowned in a Bathtub During a Seizure

a found poem

She had had no attack for months.

Every morning she was in the saddle
by half past seven, and off to the station
for her mail. She examined the letters
and I distributed them: some to her,
some to Mr. Paine, the others to the
stenographer and myself. She dispatched
her share and then mounted her horse again
and went around superintending her farm
and her poultry the rest of the day.
Sometimes she played billiards with me
after dinner, but she was usually
too tired to play, and went early to bed.

Yesterday afternoon I told her about
some plans I had been devising while absent
in Bermuda, to lighten her burdens.
We would get a housekeeper; we would
put her share of the secretary-work
into Mr. Paine's hands.
                           No—she wasn't
willing. She had been making plans herself.
The matter ended in a compromise,
I submitted. I always did. She wouldn't
audit the bills and let Paine fill out the checks—
she would continue to attend to that
herself. Also, she would continue to be

housekeeper, and let Katy assist. Also,
she would continue to answer the letters
of personal friends for me. Such was the
compromise. Both of us called it by that
name, though I was not able to see where
my formidable change had been made.

Night is closing down; the rim of the sun
barely shows above the sky-line of the hills.

She had been long an exile from home when
she came to us three-quarters of a year ago.
She had been shut up in sanitariums,
many miles from us. How eloquent glad
and grateful she was to cross her father's
threshold again!

          Why did I build this house,
two years ago? To shelter this vast
emptiness?

Paine has just found on her desk a long list
of names—fifty, he thinks—people to whom
she sent presents last night. Apparently
she forgot no one. And Katy found there
a roll of bank-notes, for the servants.
                    And
in a closet she had hidden a surprise
for me—a thing I have often wished I owned:
a noble big globe.

Icarus, in Therapy

"As long as you tried your best,"
he'd say, as though I was fair to middling
and down in the dumps.
But I'd always get the highest grades, and once
a perfect report card: formidable
as Alpine slopes after an avalanche.
A taste of rarefied air.
I tried harder. Gold medals. The important thing,
to try. My best.
I learned to test its heights
and depths. Was prairie sky, nights
before exams, popping Wake-Ups,
forty milligrams of caffeine
in a pill smaller than a watch battery.
Laps on an empty stomach.
I hungered for the simplicity
of twenty bucks for each A, the motivation
of venture capitalists, a bottom line.
But I chained myself to trying my best
until the outcome was extraneous,
the effort so pure,
it defined my whole myth.

Eve, in the Garden

Silence is quicksand.
What you didn't say.
His face searching for words,
searching and flummoxed. You heard
small creatures—chipmunk, mouse,
gecko, vole—skedaddle into the underbrush,
clearing the path ahead of him, as he went off
to gather his thoughts.

Left to your own devices, you take an apple.
Turn it in your hand, polishing away
the bloom. It smells like new words.

You cut it, and the free half falls
over, tight as a tumbler in the Chinese circus.
Mirrored in the blade, a serrated smile.
You quarter it, and the second cut sounds
as different from the first
as one footfall from the next, the lion
and the lamb. A pithy argument, accusation.
In each quarter is the face of an owl: dark eyes
unblinking.

Pandora @ Snoops Anon.

Every box, cabinet, drawer, and vault
calls to me with breath warm as the Aegean,
sweet as honeydew. My favourite

invention: the skeleton key.
My hymn: "In Praise of Steam."

The postcard is an easy fix.
I like the risk that locks and seals invite.

I'm the one who opens the can of nuts
stuffed with a snake at the office shin-dig,

letters misdelivered to me and, once,
the journal of a fired colleague.

Some things got out.
It's not my fault.

What life is airtight?
Fingers, ears, and eyes, all hungry, all the time.

Every box, cabinet, drawer, and vault
calls to me, its song a honeyed chant:
what you want, what you want, what you want.

Babysat by Sylvia Plath

for Peter Gibian, who was

In spring, her face gerbera-bright.
On the living room carpet, scattered
pop-up books, Tinker Toy spools, sticks,
everything dappled, everything dubitative.

A cheese sandwich, lemonade
on a blanket in the shade of the poplar tree,
in summer. She connects the word *cicada*
to the live-wire sound you've often heard
but couldn't name. Then the word *lunula*
as she lifts your fingertips for "London Bridge."

In winter, gliding behind her in the sled,
you and your dark twin
erase her footprints.
Moon is rising, Bruegeling the snow.
At home, she makes you cocoa,
and forever after you thirst
for darkness, the moment
the light begins to fail.

In autumn, watch her leave, coatless,
hugging her own breakable parcel.

Glenn Gould's Chair

with five lines hacked from How to Design a Chair *(Design Museum/Conran Octopus, 2010)*

The
chair
is
a
sug-
gestive
form.
Even
un-
occupied, it recalls the human frame,
a back, a seat, and legs, sometimes arms.
To sit down (sink in?) is to stake a claim.
The curule seat. Womb. Whatever it does,
it must support the body without breaking.
First rule: support is dictated by use;
Glenn Gould's hacked bridge chair kept him just fourteen
inches off the floor, its cushion worn through
until there was only a wooden slat
to balance his rear on. So how do you
design a chair as perfect as that?
       Take saw, piano wire, duct tape, and bolts.
       Keep humming until you run out of notes.

Cry

The cup too full, tired experiment in surface tension.
The latch stuck, stuck, stuck, and then the gate

lurches open. Luxury of hot tears.
Constellation of crumpled Kleenex

on the quilted bedspread.
You awaken from a wine-induced sleep

to cardinal's song and warm floorboards,
a sliding screen door, the patched

overturned boat someone hoisted to the cove.
The blousy, stooped hedge after rain.

You've seen those lists of words
with no English translation: *saudade, litost, toska.*

To awaken, dream-
bruised, to your own life.

Sponge, on a shelf beside the bath

Forgets the words to its own song.
Obdurate, sits curled into itself
like the old soul at the Legion,
the ascetic who has already left us behind.
Come back!
Plunge it into water
to feel it fill and rise in the hand
like a heart pumping afresh,
a promise.
A Fort-Da game
in which we choose to forget
that flesh is our own song.

Violet

you blossomed below my window
when still frost crystalized mornings

you waited and rain too
sad for April fell always you

drank the rain you drank
the rain. I noticed this afternoon

the sun on lapis petals and yellow
delightful—a wink of the eye

there is nothing left for me to do
but offer my hand

Sex at Thirty-Eight

These days you whip
out of the house like a banner
in a used car lot, buffeted by to-dos,
tamping down your hunger for lack of
time, whose wingèd chariot passes you
along with the clogged bus. And just

what you need this morning:
a bottleneck at the counter
as young lovers idle and nuzzle
while she sweetens her coffee,
languorous as sex in July: two
soft pumps of the cream dispenser, flick
of the sugar packet, stir stick, kiss, sugar
falling like sand in an hourglass.

You want to doctor your espresso,
get on with it. But in the radius of
their desire, time bends: you see
the gold new whiskers on his chin,
her hair tangled and glossy,
dirt under your nail.
Swallow the urge to *ahem*.

Meet your husband in the snarl of straphangers in the train
lugging home diapers, midterms, rotisserie chicken.
Look into this stranger's face. Proposition.
Rush back to the bed you conceived your baby in,
bed that once inched across the floor.
O desire shaped by love's sweet lathe.

Happy New Ear

for Wes, and with thanks to Phoebe (age 3) for the title

Here's to fresh starts, clearing the decks,
making it new, forgiving debts. Last year
was grim. All bets were off. Needles and pins
and sink or swim. Grist for the mill and misery
loves company, a bitter pill, a monkey-
wrench in the machinery. Tooth and nail and
a leap in the dark. When it rains it pours. Listen,
here's to fresh starts.

Brisking about the Life

Must have been the people who drown them in sacks
who said cats are "independent." Mine pad behind me,
swinging the hammocks of their bellies, ready
to pitch camp in every room I sweep into. Never fails:
they Frisbee toss themselves between the mattress
and the clean sheet when they see me snap it
like a napkin under my chin. When we eat they circle
the pool of air under the table waiting
for a somebody to drop lure. It's unnerving
how the tabby with Bengal blood starts his motor
the moment I lay my hand on his upholstery.
And quick gears! Uncoiling, he lurches toward me,
claims each of my hands with his stamp-pad nose.
The ginger tabby dreams of riding in my side car,
swatting at pencils raised like the flags on country mailboxes.
They hear my step on the stair and are mid-
do-see-do when I drop my bags by the shoe-rack.
And they wheel around to pad behind me,
reciting jeremiads for the people who drown them in sacks.

Museum of Kindness

1.

There isn't one. I Googled
because my nine-year-old girl,
thumbing *Life Through the Ages*,
pointed to a double-page spread
featuring a guillotine, a condemned man
(shirtless, face-down on the bascule,
cinched by the lunette, haloed
by the straw basket set to catch his head,
beside a cart holding three other bound men)
and said, "Cool," in early-tween blasé.
Might have been a Raadvad Bread Slicer,
a few loaves of pumpernickel.
Check out the Revolutionary officers
chatting like cops ordering takeout.

2.

Museum of Medieval Torture—
for those who like to think
it doesn't happen today.

3.

Killed with kindness? *Bless your heart,*
they say in the South.

4.

Brick is more dear than breath
in this world.

Then there's the philosophical question:
what might qualify as instruments
of kindness? Welfare? Morphine?
A cup of tea, a roll of quarters
at the Soap Opera Laundromat,
a basin and a sponge?

There's still room in the suggestion box.

5.

I peel two Moroccan clementines
because my son can't peel them
himself. He'd bite into the rind, stop
loving what he now loves easily
in his chafe-charged world.

With the tip of a butter knife,
I pry out the hard, star-shaped calyx
that can puncture my probing thumb.
Then the rind—fresh spray misting
the countertop, my hands. Gently

strip off the pith like flocked wallpaper
(impatience gouges, exposes the pulp).
I want the dimpled surface,
zenith to nadir, of each sphere.
I groom it, hold it intact before

poking my thumb into the divot at the top.
Halving the fruit, I pull its thready pith
from the central axis. Segment and hold
each crescent to the light like a suitcase
on the conveyer through Security.

If he bites a seed, goodbye clementine.
Knife performs the odd lumpectomy.
In a Ziploc on an ice pack in his lunchbox,
stash the flawless lunulae, twenty little
bridges between his hands and mine.

6.

When I was 21, in Nice
and afraid to fly home,
barfing into a garbage can
on a busy sidewalk outside the Nice Etoile,
a woman, Patti-Smith-beautiful,
came up to me, asked in English,
"Are you all right?" put a clutch of Kleenex
in my palm and was gone.

7.

O common finch,
on concrete below skyscraper,
you are like only yourself.

8.

We've been invited again to our friends'
Swedish *Julpyssel*—a party to putter around
making stuff for Christmas. Gingerbread
cookies and house kits, bowls of candy,
tubes of icing and marzipan arrayed
on a crisp white cloth on the dining table.
Children stand or kneel on chairs
over their work, smearing icing on a rooftop
or cheek. Adults drink wine, scarf
open-faced salmon & dill sandwiches, or
lose themselves in avant-garde cookie art.
Our children love the festivities—
the decorate-one-eat-one sugar rush.
"Jolly," my daughter says, pressing Skittles
into icing shutters. My son slaps lampshades,
running between the Dala horses in the front room
and the sweets table. *Cobra Hands!*
a babysitter dubbed him. His one never-fail word:
again. My husband and I take turns as designated
shadow to our little runner.
                              This is his happy scream.
              I can glue that.
For our family, invitations are understandably rare.
Unwonted, Dickens or Henry James might say, knowing
something about exile and inclusion. *Each man
is a half-open door / leading to a room for everyone,*
Tranströmer wrote, in a rare show of optimism.
                    Sometimes, our host,
though he doesn't drink, makes *glögg,*
dims the lights and flames the brandy. We feel
the warmth of this ritual, as the flame shoots up

and Peter stands back, the hush
as he ladles mulled wine, raisins, almonds
into mugs, passes them down the table.

Berkeley sends us home with a plate of shortbread,
pepparkakor, lemon bars, chocolate truffles.
How can it be that, every year,
I fail to send a thank you card.

9.

There'd be a wing devoted to the best
intentions.

I think if it existed, we'd go.

Idyll

Fat flies play the didgeridoo at the kitchen windowsill.
Sprinkler throws its drink in lawn's face for the 90th take.
To each his own, says the squirrel.
The sun has managed to dodge the clouds for the better part of the day.
Two boys on the sidewalk practice whistling with the reeds of their
    fingers.
One's an expert, the other hasn't quite caught on. Ring
around the collar under fine down on their tanned necks,
dirty fingernails are *memento mori* if anyone cares to look.
I'd rather drag the hose a foot or two closer,
hearkening to the rough green notes. Spring.
        One boy has eyelashes like a daisy folded in half,
        the other, freckles in his ears.

Rosary

Look, the wind gave back to the trees their leaves.
—my daughter, four years old

The frost reunited the grass with its shawl

The cloud wed the pond to the sky

Wren gave back to the clock its song

Drain restored to water its eye

Slyly, cold turned water to stone

The wind gave back to the trees their leaves

Clock remembered its debt to time

The suitcase unzipped and yielded to dusk

The river gave back to willow its tongue

Snow startled the lake from its dream

The drought gave back to the soil its wings

The sun licked the flag dry

Rain put worm out of house and home

Fog unfastened her dress of sky

Fire requited to the house its bones

Glory be, glory be, glory be

Bonne Continuation

La vida es corta, pers archa. (Life is short, but wide.)

In the métro, a guy with a shaved head is wearing pants featuring vertical stripes and a sweater with horizontal stripes, and a person remarks aloud, "That's a lot of stripes for a bald guy."

Ideas for names for Ted's yearling filly, by Cozzene (sire) and Suivez-là: Scene Stealer, Last Seen, Runaway Cousin, Moll Flanders, Là-Voilà, Follow Coz, Lady Zenith, Sweet Rocket, Cousin Swifty, La Sprezzatura, Cosmopolite, Cosmic String, Costume Drama, Suasion, Comblance.

Complexify.

Overheard at the outdoor pool on the mountain: "Fix your bathing suit. Or someone might start calling you a slut." Said by a boy of about twelve, to his younger sister. Later (to a man who might be his uncle): "Your pocket. It's sticking out. My god, did you see that butterfly?"

Aureole of blooms on late garden phlox.

An apple bruised on one cheek.
A lip-gloss kiss left on elevator brass.

La Sprezzatura is the name he chose.

Light caramelizing there.
A heart of blown glass.

Stuff in André Breton's studio: a picture of men fencing, metal boomerangs, amulets, stuffed Pekinese dog head, stones, fish, blood-red coral, vitrine containing exotic birds, *Portrait d'Alfred Jarry* (by Cazals).

In the métro, a woman holding a water bottle like a shot-put under her chin, against her cheek.

A fragment of ash in your coffee jumps away from your fingertip.

When do we turn back the clocks?

Acknowledgements and Notes

I gratefully acknowledge the support of the Canada Council for the Arts, which assisted in the development of this work (under its working title "Genre") in the form of a grant for Professional Writers (awarded in 2008).

Tremendous thanks to my family: to Wes, for your love, partnership, feedback, and support, and to our children, for the burnishing.

To the top-notch team at Brick—my outstanding editor Alayna Munce, acquisitions editor Barry Dempster, my book's copy editor Maureen Scott Harris, the wonderful Kitty Lewis, the book designer Marijke Friesen—thank you for helping to make this a Brick Book.

Thanks to René Bolduc for the arresting cover photograph, *Simon-Geai-Bleu*, which I first saw exhibited at Dawson College.

Marge Piercy's feedback and critique helped to strengthen some of these poems. I worked with Marge during her Poetry Intensive Workshop in Wellfleet, Massachusetts, in 2013.

Deep thanks to these careful readers and dear friends: Rachel Rose, Masarah Van Eyck, Stephanie Bolster, Sarah Venart, Andrew Katz. Rachel & Isabelle; Masarah & Mike; Janet & Bill; Erin & Mark; Berkeley & Peter; Maggie & Brian: you and your families each have a wing in my museum of kindness. The poem "Museum of Kindness" is for Berkeley Kaite & Peter Ohlin and Maggie Kilgour & Brian Trehearne, who for several years have shared their holidays, hospitality, and friendship with us.

To my siblings, Janet, Debbie, and Bill: thanks for inspiring or giving feedback on poems in the manuscript.

Thanks to Emma Gerlach, Talya Bromley, Gabrielle Thomas, Cassandra Monette, Alice Boom, Bianca Brunetti, Rafael Finn, and Jacqueline Whyte Appleby—my children's babysitters—and to all of the folks at Eleanor Côté Home, for their attentive care work, which freed me in short spurts to work on poems or dishes or sleep over the past eight years.

Some of these poems have been previously published (sometimes in different versions) in other publications or have had previous lives:

"Box" was selected by Poet Laureate John Steffler as winner of the 2007 *Arc Poetry Magazine* poem of the year prize. It appeared in the *Best Canadian Poetry in English 2008*, and in *The Best of the Best Canadian Poetry* (2017).

"Crossing Over," a version of "Poetry," "A Poet Has Nine Knives," and "Rosary" were longlisted in the 2014 Canada Writes: CBC Poetry Prize competition.

"The Tenants" appeared in the Montreal issue of *The New Quarterly* (2008).

"Convalescent" was first published in *I, Nadja, and Other Poems* (Brick, 2006).

"Faith Is a Suitcase," "A Poet Has Nine Knives," "Unteachable Moment," "If," "Conventions," "Ativan," and "Descent" appeared online in *Numéro Cinq*.

Versions of "Legacy" and "Violet" appeared in *When Your Body Takes to Trembling* (Cranberry Tree, 1996).

"Event Horizon" appeared in *Arc Poetry Magazine* and was an Editor's Choice selection for the poem of the year contest in 2013.

"In Praise of Hospital Cafeterias" was shortlisted in the *PRISM International* poetry competition, and was published in the journal (2014).

"Gift Horse" appeared in the *Best Canadian Poetry, 2015*. "Gift Horse" and "My Daughter, Crying Herself to Sleep" (published as "A Khanga for

My Daughter, Crying Herself to Sleep") appeared in *The New Quarterly* (2014). These poems were shortlisted in the magazine's Occasional Verse contest.

"Icarus, in Therapy" was published in 2014, as part of the Dusie Blog Tuesday poem series, the offshoot, curated by rob mclennan, of the Swiss online journal *Dusie*.

"Eve, in the Garden" (originally titled "Ripe"), "Pandora @ Snoops Anon." (originally titled "Snoop") and "Babysat by Sylvia Plath" (presented together as an "irresistible triptych") were broadcast on the CBC as part of the 2006 Poetry Face-Off Competition.

"Glenn Gould's Chair" was longlisted in the 2015 University of Canberra's Vice-Chancellor's International Poetry Prize and appeared in the anthology, *Underneath*.

"Brisking about the Life" was selected by John Steffler to be a Parliamentary Poet's Poem of the Month, online.

"*Bonne Continuation*" (originally titled "*Bonne Continuation*: A List of Random Jottings from My Notebook") appeared in the List Issue, guest-edited by Diane Schoemperlen, of *The New Quarterly* (2010). Some lines have been borrowed from my poem titled "Montreal: Views of the City," commissioned by Montreal poet laureate Martin Thibault for a vernissage in 2014 at La Galerie Beaux-arts des Amériques.

———

In the poem "Genre," the phrase "Doing It Right with Rona" is the slogan of an ad campaign for the Rona hardware store.

The title of the poem "*But the mob all calls me 'Swingin'-Door Susie*'" comes from the 1938 film, *Bringing Up Baby*, starring Carey Grant and Katherine Hepburn.

The title of the poem "*Now you can turn your personal gear into an on-the-go bullet-proof shield*" is advertising copy for the LifePlate™ Discrete

Personal Bullet-Proof Insert for backpacks, bags, and briefcases. The LifePlate™ was invented by high-school student Lauren Sorge, after she experienced a lockdown at her school.

The italicized lines in "Happy Blues" are from Ella Fitzgerald's song of the same name.

The found poem "Charles Darwin on His Namesake, Charles Waring Darwin" is from J. David Smith's 1999 article, "Darwin's Last Child: Mental Retardation and the Need for a Romantic Science" (*Mental Retardation*: December 1999, Vol. 37, No. 6, pp. 504–506). Parslow was the Darwins' butler.

The found poem "Mark Twain, December 25, 1909, on the Death of His Daughter Jean, Who Drowned in a Bathtub During a Seizure" is from "The Death of Jean" in *What Is Man and Other Essays*.

Susan Elmslie's first trade collection of poetry, *I, Nadja, and Other Poems* (Brick, 2006), won the A. M. Klein Poetry Prize and was short-listed for the McAuslan First Book Prize, the Pat Lowther Award, and a ReLit Award. Her poems have also appeared in several journals and anthologies—including the *Best Canadian Poetry in English* (2008, 2015, and 2017)—and in a prize-winning chapbook, *When Your Body Takes to Trembling* (Cranberry Tree, 1996). A Hawthornden Poetry Fellow, she holds an MA in Canadian Literature from Western and a PhD in English from McGill. She currently teaches English literature and creative writing at Dawson College in Montreal.